*LAMASERY OF
HARMONY AND PEACE*

雍和宫

FOREIGN LANGUAGES PRESS BEIJING
外文出版社　北京

LAMASERY OF HARMONY AND PEACE

Yonghegong is located inside Andingmen in the northeastern part of Beijing. Built in 1694, the 33rd year of the reign of Emperor Kangxi, it was at first the mansion of Yinzhen, the emperor's fourth son, who later succeeded to the throne and became Emperor Yongzheng. In 1725, the third year of Emperor Yongzheng, the mansion became the emperor's secondary palace and was renamed the Palace of Harmony and Peace. In 1744, the ninth year of Emperor Qianlong's reign, the palace was converted into a lamaist temple, which also served as the administrative centre of Buddhist affairs of the Qing government.

The Mongolian and Tibetan peoples have been two important ethnic minorities since historical times. For the stability of the regime and peace at the borders, it was necessary for the Qing court to exercise control over them by every means. As most of the Mongolians and Tibetans were believers in the lamaist form of Buddhism, Emperor Qianlong encouraged the spread of the Yellow Sect of Lamaism in the interior and led the imperial family in following the creed so as the maintain a close link with the areas inhabited by the Mongolians and Tibetans. As he also made frequent contact with the leading lamas, such as Dalai and Panchen, and leading Mongolian monks, he was supported by their followers in keeping the country and people in peace and security. It was against this background that Yonghegong was converted into a lamaist temple.

The grounds of Yonghegong measure nearly 400 metres from north to south and 50-80 metres from east to west. There are altogether 1134 rooms in the temple buildings, totalling 23131.8 square metres in floor space. The principal structures in Yonghegong include three monumental arches, the Gate of Harmony and Peace (Yonghemen), Hall of Harmony and Peace (Yonghedian), Hall of Eternal Blessings (Yongyoudian), Hall of the Wheel of Dharma (Falundian) and Hall of Infinite Happiness (Wanfuge), which stand in five courtyards, one behind another. There are also the auxiliary side halls, the four halls of learning (Scripture-Lecturing Hall, Esoteric Hall, Mathematics Hall and Bhaisajya Hall), the Initiation Terrace and Panchen's Tower. The courtyards are progressively reduced in size from the south to the north while the buildings rise progressively higher, giving people an enigmatic impression, the impression of a place "where dragons and phoenixes gather." Since the predecessor of Yonghegong was the mansion of a prince and the emperor's secondary palace, the structures bear the architectural characteristics of palace structures and Tibetan temple buildings. This is most prominent in the Hall of the Wheel of the Dharma and the Hall of Infinite Happiness. The Hall of the Wheel of the Dharma is the great central hall where the lamas gather to perform Buddhist rituals. The Hall of Infinite Happiness enshrines the Great Buddha Maitreya .All of the names of the Yonghegong buildings and inscriptions on the stone stelae in the lamasery are in four languages: Han, Manchu, Mongolian and Tibetan. This not only is in harmony with the architectural style, but also shows how much thought Emperor Qianlong had given to maintaining the unity and unification of the multi-national country.

    Preserved in Yonghegong is a rich collection of cultural relics, particularly those related to Tibetan Buddhism. In addition to the large number of vividly sculptured Buddhist statues, each different in posture and expression, there are also a large collection of Tibetan-style paintings known as Tangka paintings, murals, scriptures and religious instruments and vessels. The inscriptions on the stelae and boards, the paintings and calligraphic works, decorations and ornaments in the lamasery are also of very high cultural and historical value. *The Hill of 500 Arhats* carved in red sandalwood, the Buddha's shrine carved in golden-striped Nanmu hardwood and the giant Buddha carved in white sandalwood are known as the three masterpieces of wood carving in Yonghegong. In 1750, after the revolt staged by the Tibetan local chieftain Jurmod was put down by an army of the Qing government sent by Emperor Qianlong, the military and administrative powers in Tibet were placed in the hands of the seventh Dalai Lama. To repay the emperor's favour, the seventh Dalai Lama obtained a white sandalwood tree trunk for the emperor from Nepal through exchange with a large quantity of gems. When the log was shipped to Yonghegong, Emperor Qianlong appointed Living Buddha Charhan to oversee the designing and carving of it into a statue of the Buddha. The Hall of Infinite Happiness, in which the giant Buddha is enshrined, was built after the giant Buddha was completed. This gave rise to the saying: The giant Buddha came before Yonghegong. The Buddhist shrine and sandalwood Buddha are in the Hall of Buddha's Light. Empress Dowager Niugulu was said have a gold crown of 70-percent purity weighing more than 10 kilogrammes made for the statue and a large and rare luminous pearl inlaid on the forehead of the statue. It is to be regretted that both were lost in the early half of this century.

During the most flourishing period in history, the temple was staffed by more than 500 lamas. There are nearly 90 of them today and most of them are from Inner Mongolia and Fuxin in the Northeast. Kabuyang Tubudan, the present abbot of Yonghegong, is a lama of profound learning and a holder of the Gexi academic degree. He not only has a thorough knowledge about the Mongolian and Tibetan scriptures, but also is well versed in Sanskrit. In recent years, he has collaborated with others in translating and publishing several monumental works, including the translation of the *Great Compendium of Sutras* from Tibetan into Mongolian and the Mongolian edition of the *Four-Volume Medical Classic.* Luosang Samadan is the most favorite disciple of Tubudan. Entering the temple at 15, he is now the vice-abbot. In addition to his heavy work load, he is at present compiling a scriptural textbook for the lamas to recite every day.

Monks in Yonghegong observe the regulations and disciplines of the Yellow Sect of Tibetan Buddhism, a statue of the Great Master Zongkaba, founder of the Geru Sect, is enshrined in the Hall of the Wheel of the Dharma, where the monks in cassocks perform rituals and chant scriptures every morning. During religious festivals and on memorial days, Buddhist activities and prayer sessions are held in the temple. In their scriptural study courses, the lamas in the temple closely observe the order that the scriptures of the Prakaranna Sect are studied before those of the Esoteric Sect.

The Buddhist religious affairs in Yonghegong are supervised by the Temple Administrative Committee formed by lamas and with the posts of abbot and supervisors on the committee. In the Qing Dynasty, the abbot and vice-abbot were appointed by the court, and the masters of the various halls and other temple officials, selected and appointed by the Dalai and Panchen lamas. The first abbot of Yonghegong was Living Buddha Changja Robidoji the Third, who concurrently held of post of chief of the Printing Department of the Lamas in the capital. The post was later filled by Mongolian lamas in most cases.

In the early 1990s, the wooden statue of Maitreya Buddha in the Hall of Infinite Happiness was repaired and gilded for the first time in more than 240 years after its completion. Upon completion in 1993, a hallowing ceremony was held in the temple. The ceremony lasted three days and was unprecedented and the largest in scale in the history of Yonghegong. There was also a incinerating ceremony. Buddhist rules require it that before a statue is to be repaired, the Buddha it represents must be sent away by chanting scriptures to reduce the statue into an unholy piece of wood so that the Buddha will not be offended by any work done to the statue. After the repair is done, the Buddha is invited back or hallowed. After the hallowing, the statue is only to be worshipped. Any improper act towards it will be a crime.

The Devil-Catching Ceremony is held in Yonghegong every year between the 29th day of the first lunar month and the first day of the second lunar month. The Devil-Catching Dance, a Buddhist religious dance, is performed during the ceremony by lamas masquerading as devils and ghosts and wearing masks. The Devil in the Devil-Catching Dance refers to the evil King Langdarma, who tried to destroy Buddhism in Tibetan history. The Devil-Catching Dance is the most characteristic religious dance to be performed in Yonghegong. The arena is set up in the courtyard of the Devaraja Hall (Gate of Harmony and Peace). The Devil-Catching Dance Ceremony lasts three days. The climax is reached on the afternoon of the second day. In the Qing Dynasty, the ceremony was attended by the emperor, princes and senior court officials. The traditional Devil-Catching Ceremony in Yonghegong was suspended for a time after 1957 and did not resume until 1988.

雍 和 宫

雍和宫位于北京市东北的安定门内,始建于康熙三十三年(1694年),原为康熙帝第四子胤禛(即后来的雍正帝)的府邸。雍正三年(1725年)提升为行宫,改名雍和宫。乾隆九年(1744年)改建为喇嘛庙,并成为清政府管理佛教事务的中心。

在中国历史上,蒙、藏一直是占有重要地位的少数民族,清王朝为了政权的巩固和边疆的安宁,就必须利用各种手段对其进行控制。而蒙、藏族大都信仰喇嘛教,于是乾隆在内地大兴黄教,皇家带头信仰,藉此沟通与蒙、藏地区的联系,保持与达赖、班禅和蒙古高僧的频繁往来,使众心归向,国泰民安。雍和宫正是在这样的背景下才改建为喇嘛庙的。

雍和宫南北长近400米,东西宽50－80米,总建筑面积23131.8平方米,共有殿堂1134间。主要建筑有三座牌坊和雍和门、雍和宫殿、永佑殿、法轮殿、万福阁等五进大殿,还有东西配殿、"四学殿"(讲经殿、密宗殿、数学殿、药师殿)和戒台楼、班禅楼等。院落从南到北空间渐次缩小,而建筑物却渐次升高,给人以"聚龙窝凤"、"高深莫测"之感。因雍和宫的前身曾贵为王府和帝王行宫，所以它的建筑兼有皇家建筑和藏式寺院的特色，尤以法轮殿和万福阁最为突出。法轮殿是雍和宫的中心大殿，是僧侣们集会或举行佛事活动的场所。万福阁是供奉弥勒大佛的殿宇。此外，庙内几乎所有宫殿的匾额、碑文都是用汉、满、蒙、藏四种文字书写，这不仅与建筑风格相协调，也体现了乾隆帝要维护多民族国家团结统一的良苦用心。

雍和宫内的文物尤其是藏传佛教文物十分丰富，各殿内不仅有大量造型生动、神态各异的佛像，还有许多唐卡、壁画、经卷、法物、法器等。另外，庙内的碑文、匾额、字画及饰物等也有很高的文物价值。紫檀木雕刻"五百罗汉山"、金丝楠木雕刻的佛龛、白檀木雕刻的大佛被誉为雍和宫"木雕三绝"。其中木雕大佛是用一整棵白檀木雕刻而成的。1750年乾隆皇帝派兵平定了西藏郡王朱尔默特的叛乱，并把西藏的军政大权交给了第七世达赖喇嘛，达赖为了报答皇恩，特用大量珍宝从尼泊尔换回这棵白檀木相送。白檀木运到雍和宫后，乾隆命察罕活佛亲自设计。大佛雕好后，再度身建造万福阁，因此，曾流传"先有大佛，后有雍和宫"的说法。金丝楠木精雕而成的佛龛和旃檀佛在照佛楼内，钮祜禄氏皇太后当年还为旃檀佛打制了一顶10多公斤重、七成金的五佛冠，并在佛像前额上镶嵌了一颗罕见的大毫光珠，可惜这两件珍贵文物均在本世纪上半叶丢失。

历史上雍和宫喇嘛最多时曾达到500余人，现有近90人，绝大部分来自内蒙古和东北阜新等地。雍和宫现任住持加木杨·吐布丹，是一位造诣高深的高僧，获有"格西"学位。他不但精通蒙、藏文经咒，尚擅长梵文。近年来，他与人合作整理出版了藏文译蒙文的《大藏经》和蒙古文版的《四部医典》等几部巨著。罗桑·撒玛丹，是吐布丹最得意的弟子，他15岁入寺，现为副住持。在繁忙的工作之余，他还编写了供僧侣们诵经用的日诵课本。

雍和宫僧侣严格遵循黄教律规。法轮殿内供奉着格鲁派创始人宗喀巴上师的法像，每天清晨，僧侣们都要身穿袈裟到佛像前礼拜、诵经；宗教节日或纪念日都要举行佛事活动和法会；寺中喇嘛学经严格遵循先显宗后密宗的次第。

雍和宫的佛教事务由僧侣组成的寺庙管理委员会负责，设有住持、副住持、管家等职。清代，住持须经朝廷委任，其他各殿主师则由达赖、班禅从西藏堪布厅选派。第一位住持由京城喇嘛印务处主任三世章嘉·若必多吉活佛兼任，以后大都由蒙古族喇嘛担任。

九十年代初，雍和宫寺庙管理委员会对万福阁内的木雕大佛进行修缮贴金，这是大佛造成后240多年来的第一次。1993年工程告竣，寺内举行了隆重的开光庆典。开光活动共进行了三天，其规模和盛况在雍和宫的历史上是空前的，且第一次举行了"烧施"法会。根据佛家仪轨，佛像修缮前需要先诵经把佛送走，这样佛像就成了一根没有神灵的木头，人们修缮时的任何动作都不会冒犯它。待修缮完毕后，需要把佛请回来，迎神安住，即"开光"。开光后的佛像人们只能顶礼膜拜，任何非礼动作都被视为罪过。

雍和宫一年一度的"打鬼"活动，在每年农历正月二十九至二月初一举行。"打鬼"藏语称"跳布扎"，是僧侣身着鬼神服装头戴面具表演的一种佛教舞蹈。这里的"鬼"主要是指西藏历史上毁灭佛法的恶王朗达尔玛。"打鬼"是雍和宫最具特色的宗教仪式，坛场设在天王殿（即雍和门）前的庭院中。持续三天的"打鬼"活动在第二天下午达到高潮，在清代，皇帝和王公大臣也来观看。1957年后雍和宫传统的"打鬼"仪式曾一度中断，到1988年得以重新恢复。

Yonghegong is composed of seven courtyards arrange along a single axis. The courtyards are progressively reduced in size one after another from south to north while the structures rise progressively higher, giving one the impression of infinite height and depth and exemplifying the traditional Chinese style of architecture, which emphasizes "opening the gates to the sun and concealing the rows of buildings behind them".

雍和宫的七进院落从南到北渐次缩小,而建筑物渐次升高,体现了中国"正殿高大而重院深藏"、"宫门向阳而层层掩护"的传统建筑风格。

There are three monumental arches in Yonghegong, standing on the east, west and north sides of the first courtyard. Built in 1744, the ninth year of Emperor Qianlong, the original structures with columns and beams were regrettably stolen during the Japanese war of aggression against China and replaced with concrete ones as we see them today.

雍和宫牌楼，共有三座，分立于第一进院落的东、西、北面，建于乾隆九年（1744年），原来梁柱均采用名贵的金丝楠木构筑，底座为叶青石。可惜日军在侵华战争期间，偷偷将原梁柱拆走，代之以水泥梁柱。如今，人们见到的就是被偷梁换柱后的牌楼。

Above Right: A carved design of auspicious dragon and phoenix and sets of brackets on one of the monumental arches.

右上图为牌楼上雕刻的龙凤呈祥图案和斗拱层叠的造型。

On the side wall of the gate structure is a design carved in relief of two dragons sporting pearls with the character for "longevity" between them, which symbolizes blessing and a long life.

门两侧墙上的浮雕采用二龙戏珠并嵌有"寿"字图案,寓意"福寿双降"。

The Gate of Luminous Peace (Zhaotaimen), the entrance to the second courtyard, is a structure of three gateways. As the walls and roofs are decorated with yellow and green glazed bricks and tiles, the gate is also called the Glazed Gate.

昭泰门,是雍和宫第二进院落的大门,共有三座门楼,因采用黄色、绿色的琉璃护壁、盖顶,所以又称琉璃门。

Behind the Gate of Luminous Peace are the Bell and Drum Towers standing on the eastern and western sides of the courtyard. First built in 1744, the ninth year of Emperor Qianlong's reign, in the architectural style of multiple eaves and hipped-gable roofs, the two towers are decorated with golden and painted designs. Picture shows an outside view of the Bell Tower.

分列于昭泰门内东、西两侧的钟楼和鼓楼,始建于乾隆九年(1744年),采用重檐歇山式结构,环以描金彩绘的外廊。图为钟楼外景。

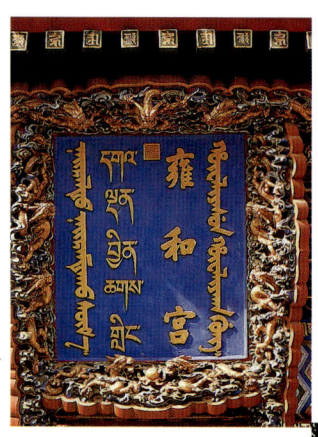

The Imperial Stele Pavilion. The essay, "On Lamas", written by ▷ Emperor Qianlong, is carved on the four sides of the stele in the pavilion in the Han, Manchu, Mongolian and Tibetan languages. The Han-language version is in the hand of Emperor Qianlong himself. The stele has become an important object for the study of the ethnic and religious policies of the Qing dynasty.

御碑亭,亭内石碑四面分别用汉、满、蒙、藏文镌刻乾隆所撰《喇嘛说》全文,其中汉文为乾隆御笔。此碑文成为研究清代民族、宗教政策的重要史料。

The name of the Hall of Harmony and Peace on the board is in the handwriting of Emperor Qianlong in the Han, Manchu, Mangolian and Tibetan languages.

雍和宫殿匾额。为乾隆御笔,用汉、满、蒙、藏四种文字书写。

The Gate of Harmony and Peace is eternally enshrouded in the smoke of burning incense. Originally the front entrance to the Mansion of Prince Yong, it was renamed the Devaraja Hall for the four heavenly kings enshrined there after the mansion was converted into a lamasery.

雍和门前常年香烟氤氲。雍和门原为雍亲王府大门,改庙以后,成为天王殿,内供四大天王。

Inside the Hall of the Wheel of the Dharma.
法轮殿内景。

The Hall of the Wheel of the Dharma is built on a cross-shaped plane. There are five dormer windows on the roof decorated with gilded bronze pinnacles.

法轮殿平面呈十字形,殿顶上建有 5 座天窗式的暗楼,并饰以五座铜质镏金宝塔。

The Hall of the Wheel of the Dharma is the main building of Yonghegong and an important place where the lamas lecture on the scriptures and hold other religious activities. It is a building of seven bays in width and five bays in depth. It is brightened by five dormer windows in the roof, each decorated with a gilded pinnacle. This kind of buildings with pinnacles on top are richly characteristic of the temples of Tibetan Buddhism.

法轮殿,为雍和宫的主体建筑,是喇嘛们讲经说法、举行佛事活动的重要场所。面宽七间,殿前后各出抱厦五间。该殿的顶部开辟了五个天窗,每个天窗之上都装饰有镏金宝顶,带有浓厚的藏传佛教寺院的特征。

The caisson ceiling of the Hall of Harmony and Peace. Corresponding to the Hall of the Buddha in other temples, the Hall of Harmony and Peace was originally the main hall, the Hall of Silvery Peace, in the Mansion of Prince Yong. Its imperial style of architecture and interior and exterior decorations can be seen in its caisson ceiling.

雍和宫殿藻井。雍和宫殿相当于寺中的大雄宝殿,因它原是雍亲王府的正殿——银安殿,所以建筑格局与内外装饰都富有皇家气派,由此藻井便可见一斑。

Panchen's Tower on the eastern side of the Hall of the Wheel of the Dharma was built in 1779, the 44th year of Emperor Qianlong, on the original site of the Terrace of Bhaisajya Buddha for the sixth Panchen Lama to stay and engage in religious rituals during his visit to Beijing. The building was opened to public in 1984 as an exhibition hall of religious art.

班禅楼,位于法轮殿东侧。乾隆四十四年(1779年)为迎接六世班禅进京,将原来的药师坛拆除改建成此楼,供六世班禅作为安禅、弘法的场所。1984年后,这里被辟为宗教艺术陈列室对外开放。

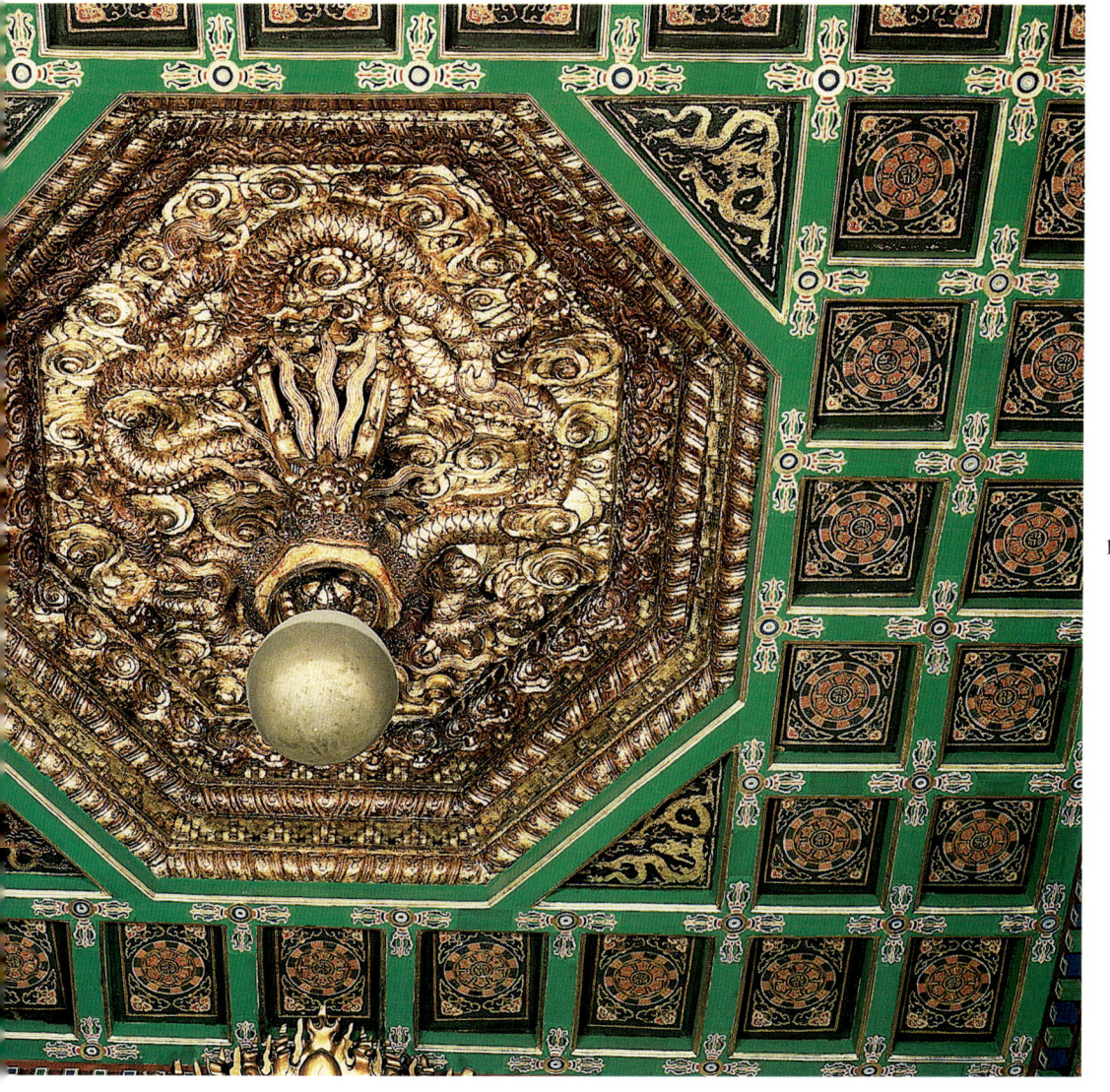

Two overhead passages connect the hall and pavilions and turn them into a structure like the buildings in a fairy tale.

两廊凌空，将三座殿阁连为一体，宛如仙阁。

Architectural details of the Hall of Infinite Happiness.
万福阁局部造型

The Hall of Infinite Happiness, also known as the Tower of the Giant Buddha, is 30 metres high with three layers of upturned eaves. The Pavilion of Eternal Health (Yongkangge) and Pavilion of Perpetual Tranquility (Yansuige) flanking it on the left and right are connected to it by overhead passages. Very few buildings in this architectural style of the Liao and Kin periods still exist today.

万福阁又名大佛楼，高30米，飞檐三重。永康阁和延绥阁分列左右，中间有悬空的飞廊相连，具有辽金建筑风格，现存极少。

The shrine of golden-striped Nanmu hardwood in the Tower of Buddha's Light is one of the three masterpieces of wood carving in Yonghegong. The pillars of the three-sectioned shrine are carved with 99 coiling dragons. The standing statue of Sakyamuni carved in sandalwood in the Ming dynasty is flanked by Ananda and Kasyapa.

雍和宫木雕三绝之一——照佛楼的金丝楠木佛龛。采用龙抱柱造型,分内外三层,雕刻99条云龙。龛内供奉明代旃檀释迦牟尼佛站立像,两侧分别是阿难和迦叶。

The statue of Maitreya carved with the whole trunk of a white sandalwood tree is 18 metres high with another eight metres of it below the ground level. The carving of this giant wooden statue, which is very rare in China and even in the world, cost a total of 80,000 ounces of silver. The robe draped on the giant Buddha was made with 1,800 square metres of yellow satin.

木雕大佛,地上像高18米,地下8米,用整棵白檀香木雕刻而成,是现今所知中国乃至世界罕见的木雕佛像。雕刻此佛当年共花费八万两白银,仅大佛身上的一件袍子,就用黄缎1800米。

The three statues in the Hall of Eternal Blessings are carved in white sandalwood and about 2.35 metres high. They are Bhaisajya on the left, Amitayus in the middle and Buddha of the Roaring Lion on the right.

供于永佑殿的三尊佛像，系用白檀木雕刻而成，高约2.35米，左为药师佛，中为无量寿佛，右为狮吼佛。

This bronze statue of Zongkaba (1357–1419), founder of the Geru Sect of Tibetan Buddhism, is 6.1 metres high. The casting of the statue in 1924 took two years and cost 200,000 silver dollars.

宗喀巴上师像，铜胎，高6.1米，造于1924年，耗资20万银元，历时两年才完成。宗喀巴（1357－1419年）为藏语系佛教格鲁派创始人。

This 50-centimetre-high statue of Sakyamuri of gilded bronze is enshrined in front of the statue of Zongkaba in the Hall of the Wheel of the Dharma. There are Emperor Qianlong's words of exaltation on the back of the Halo. The statue, which used to be the principal Buddhist image in the hall, was for more than 200 years mistakenly believed to be one of pure gold.

供奉于法轮殿宗喀巴像前的释迦牟尼佛像，高50厘米，铜质镀金，佛像背光上有乾隆书写的赞语。以前曾是法轮殿的主佛像，曾被当作金佛像误传二百多年。

25

The 18 Arhats in the Hall of Harmony and Peace are nearly 250 years old and still shine with a golden hue. They are said to have been made by the "gold-revealing" method. After the statues of the arhats were sculptured, they were covered with goldleaf and then painted in colour. When the paint was dry, the parts with designs under them are removed gently with a knife to expose the gold underneath. This technique has become lost in China today.

十八罗汉像供奉在雍和宫殿内，至今已有近250年的历史，但仍金光熠熠。据说这是采用"拨金术"塑造的，即佛像塑成后，全身贴上一层赤金，然后再涂上一层颜料，等颜料干后，在需显露图案的部位用刀把表层的颜料轻轻拨掉，打底的贴金便显露出来。目前此术在中国已经失传。

Enshrined facing the door in the Hall of Harmony and Peace, is a statue of Sakyamuni with Maitreya on the eastern side and Dipamkara on the western side. All the three statues are nearly two metres high.

雍和宫殿的正面供有三尊高近2米的铜质佛像,释迦牟尼佛居中,西首为燃灯佛,图为东首佛像弥勒佛。

The big-pouched Maitreya of gilded wood sits on a throne of golden lacquer and carved dragons in the Devaraja Hall and greets believers and visitors with a big smile on his face.

天王殿内,木雕贴金大肚弥勒佛端坐在正中的金漆雕龙宝座上,笑迎信众与游客。

The statue of Skanda carved in wood in the Devaraja Hall is 1.76 metres high. Skanda is said to be the guardian of the pagoda of Sakyamun's relics. In all Buddhist temples, the statue of Skanda always stands facing north in the rear part of the first hall to serve as the guardian of the Dharma in the temple.

天王殿内的韦驮像,高176厘米、木质。据传,韦驮原是释迦牟尼舍利塔的护卫者。在所有寺庙中,韦驮像总是供在第一进大殿的后部、面北而立,充任庙宇的护法神。

The Hill of 500 Arhats carved in red sandalwood in the Hall of the Dharma is nearly 5 metres high, 3.5 metres wide and 0.3 metre deep. The 500 arhats, each 10 centimetres high, are cast in gold, silver, bronze, iron or tin.

法轮殿内的木雕五百罗汉山,高近5米,宽3.5米,厚30厘米,用紫檀木雕刻而成。五百罗汉分别采用金、银、铜、铁、锡制成,每个高10厘米。

The bronze tripod in front of the Hall of Harmony and Peace, 4.2 metres in height, was cast by the Construction Department of the Qing palace in 1747, the 12th year of Emperor Qianlong. It is one of the only two tripods of similar shape and designs in the country. (The other one is in the Imperial Garden of the former Imperial Palace.) Incense was burned in this tripod every time a Qing emperor came to Yonghegong to worship the Buddha.

雍和宫内的古铜鼎炉,高4.2米,铸造于乾隆十二年(1747年),为清宫养心殿造办处的制品。与此鼎造型、纹饰相似的在全国仅存两座(另一座在故宫御花园)。据说清帝每次来雍和宫拜佛,都要在此炉进香。

This bronze Sumeru Hill in front of the Hall of Harmony and Peace is 1.5 metres high and of seven tiers. Cast during the Wanli reign of the Ming dynasty, it cleverly combines religious doctrine with natural science and is high in artistic and historical value.

青铜须弥山,置于雍和宫殿前,铸造于明万历年间,高1.5米,上下共分7层。铸造者独具匠心地把宗教学说和自然科学巧妙地融为一体,具有较高的文物价值。

The bonze lions, cast during Qianlong period, ▷ in front of the Gate of Harmony and Peace have two bells and three tassels under the neck. They are the only ones of the kind in the whole country.

雍和门前的青铜狮子,铸造于乾隆年间,脖子上系有两个铜铃、三个缨络,腿部雕有鳞片,这在全国独一无二。

The Esoteric statue of the Vajra Guardian of Great Might and Virtue in the Eastern Side Hall is a statue of two figures in each other's arms. The woman in his arms is the Ming imperial concubine Luolangzawa. This Buddhist double statue symbolizes the supreme state of yoga. The male stands for wisdom, and the female, for Dhyana, or deep meditation. When the two are joined, the highest state of cultivation is attained, which is called the joining of wisdom and Dhyara.

东配殿内供奉的密宗佛像之一大威德金刚。像呈双体拥抱状，所拥抱的明妃为罗浪杂娃。在佛教中，这种双尊佛是修持到无上瑜伽部时的一种象征，男性代表智慧，女性代表禅定，两者内涵的结合达到修持的最高境界，即定慧双修。

There are five Esoteric statues in the Eastern Side Hall with the Vajra Guardian of Great Might and Virtue at the centre flanked by the Eternal Guardian of the Dharma, Heavenly Mother of Auspicity, Master of Hell and Heavenly King of Wealth. Picture shows the statue of the Master of Hell.

东配殿内供有五尊密宗造像，大威德金刚居中，永保护法、吉祥天母、地狱主和财宝天王分列左右。此像为地狱主。

A gold vase and ivory divination slips for deciding the boy who is the reincarnation of the Living Buddha were made by an imperial decree of Emperor Qianlong in 1792. This vase of pure gold of 34 centimetres in height has a duplicate kept in the Jokham Monastery in Tibet.

1792年清乾隆皇帝命制金瓶和象牙签供认定活佛转世灵童掣签用。瓶为纯金制作,高34厘米,一式两尊分供于西藏大昭寺和雍和宫。此为供于雍和宫内的金瓶。

The fish-dragon transformation tub in the Hall of the Wheel of the Dharma is also known as "the third-day tub", because Emperor Qianlong was said to have bathed in the tub three days after his birth. The broad-bean-shaped tub of golden-striped Namnu hardwood is plated with gold leaf and carved with four carp in relief to imply that the emperor was to be transformed into a true dragon ascending to the Ninth Heaven.

法轮殿内的鱼龙变化盆,又名"洗三盆",据说乾隆皇帝出生三天后曾在此盆洗过澡。盆用金丝楠木雕成,外表贴金,呈豆瓣形,浮雕了四条鲤鱼,其中一条幻化成龙,隐寓真龙天子腾达九天之意。

This big cloissone incense burner was made during the reign of Emperor Qianlong. Incense burners are placed inside or outside the halls in a temple for believers to burn incense.

景泰蓝大香炉。香炉为佛教法物、常置放于佛殿内外供信徒烧香之用。此香炉为清乾隆年间制造。

The silver Manda, also known as the Terraced City, in the Initiation Tower. The enshrining of the Manda means offering the whole universe to the Buddha.

戒台楼内的银质"曼达"。曼达又称坛城，佛门供曼达寓意为把整个宇宙献给佛菩萨。

The Tibetan-style Tangka painting of 120 × 70 centimetres in size in the Initiation Tower portrays Emperor Qianlong as a Buddha. There are Tibetan words of exaltation on the lotus-flower seat.

戒台楼内的《佛化乾隆皇帝像》唐卡高120厘米，宽70厘米。像下莲花台上题有藏文赞语。

The Five-Buddha Golden Crown preserved in the Initiation Tower is said to have been worn by Emperor Qianlong during his initiation ceremony.

藏于戒台楼内的金五佛冠，相传为乾隆皇帝受戒时所戴。

Gold-studded armour and gold-laced robe worn by Emperor Qianlong for hunting and everyday life.

清乾隆皇帝日常和行围射猎时穿用的镶金盔甲和衣袍。

The Wheel of the Dharma, conch, precious umbrella, victory pennant, lotus flower, precious vase, twin-fish and lucky knot are eight Buddhist auspicious objects, which are often placed on the table in front a Buddhist statue or used as designs on buildings. In Tibetan Buddhism, each of the eight objects has its symbolic meaning: The Wheel of the Dharma for the continuous spreading of the Buddhist doctrine in the world, the conch for the far-reaching voice of the Buddha, the precious umbrella for Buddha's protection of all things, the victory pennant for the all-conquering power of the Buddhist doctrine, the lotus flower for the purity of Buddhism uncontaminated by worldly things, the precious vase for the inexhaustible treasures to be found in Buddhism and for perfect merits and virtues, the fish for the freedom and absolution given to the world by Buddhism, and the lucky knot for linking up the boundless universe with the Buddhist doctrine.

金八瑞相、包括法轮、海螺、宝伞、胜利幢、莲花、宝瓶、双鱼、吉祥结。它们常被做成立体摆件供于佛像前或以图案形式装饰在建筑物上。在藏传佛教中，八瑞相具有深刻的宗教象征意义：法轮表示佛法永布世间；海螺表示佛音远播；宝伞表示佛能庇护万法；胜利幢表示佛法的力量战无不胜；莲花表示佛教清净而不染尘俗；宝瓶表示佛教宝藏无尽，佛法功德圆满；金鱼表示佛法能给世间自由与解脱；吉祥结表示佛教教义在大千世界中能贯穿始终。

Bells, drums and drum-sticks are Buddhist religious objects. The bell, drum and drum-stick of green jade here were used by Emperor Qianlong when chanting scriptures.

青玉铃、金刚杵、鼗鼓、均为佛教法器，用青玉制成，是乾隆皇帝诵经时所用之物。

A beautiful pagoda exquisitely woven with hair-thin gold wire.

累丝金塔,此塔亦属供物,以细如发丝的金丝制成,玲珑剔透,精巧华美。

◁ A gilded pagoda for Buddhist relics in Yonghegong.

雍和宫内供物——鎏金舍利塔。

Maitreya and Six Children. This sculpture depicting Maitreya frolicking with six children is a symbol of happiness.

弥勒与六子雕像。此雕像表现弥勒佛与六位儿童嬉戏的形态，被视为吉祥的象征。

Finely crafted conches decorated with golden ornaments. They are blown when holding Buddhist activities.

海螺，为佛教法器，此种海螺是举行佛事活动时供吹奏的，上镶嵌金属饰物，美观精制。

Silver Wheel of the Dharma. A wheel of this shape is usually placed in front of a Buddhist image. The spread of the Buddhist doctrine to save the souls of mankind is compared to the eternal forward turning of a wheel. The Buddhist doctrine is, therefore, called the Wheel of the Dharma, and preaching the Buddhist doctrine, the turning of the Wheel of the Dharma.

银制法轮,此种造型一般供奉于佛像前。因佛之说法,辗转传人,普度众生,犹如车轮永远向前,故称佛法为法轮,称佛说法为"转法轮"。

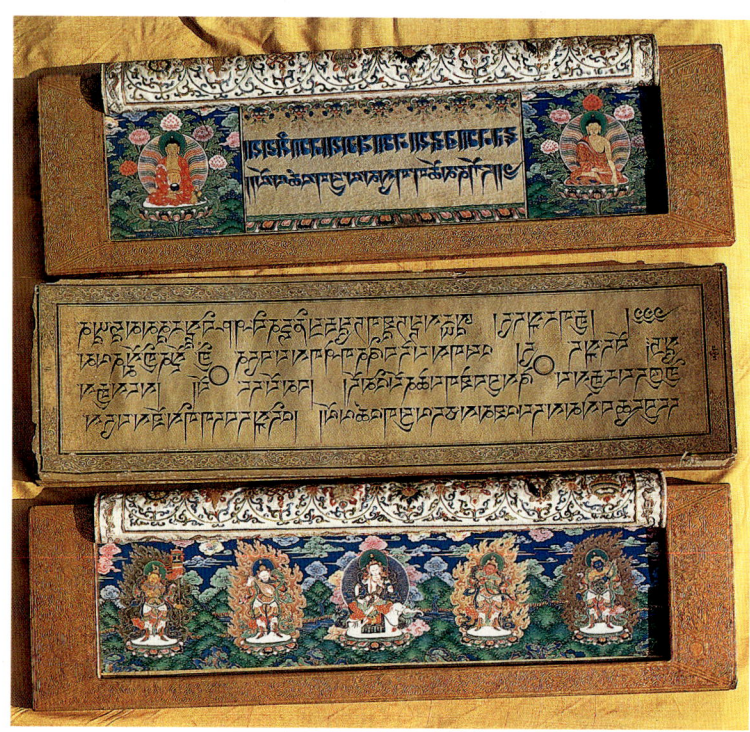

Tibetan scriptures are generally written on long, loose strips of paper, which are bound together to become a book called "strip book". All the Tibetan Buddhist canons are collected in the *Tibetan Great Compendium of Sutras*, which includes the *Ganqur Sutra* and *Danqur Sutra*. Picture shows pages from the *Canon of the Past Seven Buddhas Making Promises*. In the upper page are portraits of Sakyamuni on the left and Baisajya on the right. In the lower page is Samantabhadra Bodhisattva flanked by the Four Heavenly Kings.

藏文经典一般书写在规格相同的活页长条纸上,合并成册,被称为"长条书"。藏文经典统称《藏文大藏经》,包括《甘珠尔》和《丹珠尔》两部分。图为《过去七佛发愿分别广说经》,上页佛像左为释迦牟尼佛,右为药师佛;下页中为普贤菩萨,两边为四大天王。

Pages from the *Canon of the Great White Canopy*, also known as the *Tuoluo Canon of Mother Buddha Under the White Canopy of the Great Buddha*, which is a principal canon of the Esoteric Sect of Tibetan Buddhism.

用金汁书写的《大白伞盖经》,此经也称《大佛顶白伞盖佛母陀罗经》,为藏传佛教密乘主要经典。

The patchwork portrait of the Green Soul-Saving Mother, 2 metres long and 1.2 metres wide, was made with more than 7000 odd patches of satin of different sizes and colours. As Empress Dowager Niugulu had personally taken part in the work, the portrait has become the most valuable relic in the Hall of Eternal Blessing.

绿度母绣像，长2米、宽1.2米，是用7000多块色泽不一、大小不同的缎子补绣而成。因钮祜禄氏皇太后亲手参加了绣制，所以成了永佑殿最珍贵的文物。

◁ To celebrate the conversion of the Palace of Harmony and Peace into a temple of Tibetan Buddhism in 1745, the 10th year of Emperor Qianlong, the seventh Dalai Lama presented a set of 41 Tibetan Tangka paintings, collectively known as *Records of the Birth of the Buddha of the Citama Tree*, and wrote congratulatory words on the back of the first picture. Shown here is one of the Tangka paintings, which are preserved in perfect condition in the Hall of Infinite Happiness.

乾隆十年（1745年），七世达赖喇嘛为祝贺雍和宫改建成藏传佛教寺院，特赠送《如意宝树佛来生记》唐卡41幅，并在首幅画像背面题殊胜祝词。现在，这些唐卡完整地供奉在万福阁内，图为其中之一。

◁ A Tangka portrait of the Vajra Guardian of Great Might and Virtue, one of the gods of the Esoteric Sect of Tibetan Buddhism, who is said to be the incarnation of Manjusri Bodhisattva, whose job is to enforce Buddhist laws and suppress devils and demons with an angry face. According to Esoteric teachings, he is called the Vajra Guardian of Great Might and Virtue because he overwhelms devils and demons with great might and protects the good with great virtue. He is generally portrayed with 9 heads, 16 feet and 34 arms.

大威德金刚像(唐卡)。大威德金刚为藏传佛教密宗本尊之一,认为他是文殊菩萨的化身,以其忿怒相教令法界,降伏妖魔。按密宗教义所言,因其"有伏恶之势,谓大威 有护善之功,谓之大德",故称大威德金刚。其像一般有九头、十六足、三十四臂。

A Tangka portrait of the Silon Vajra Guardian, another god of the Esoteric Sect of Tibetan Buddhism with 4 heads, 12 arms. With the imperial concubine Ming in his arms, he is depicted with the god of desire and heretical demons under his feet to show that his duty is to drive away demons and evils.

时轮金刚像(唐卡)。时轮金刚亦是藏传佛教密宗所奉本尊像,有四头、十二臂,与明妃相拥, 脚下踩欲望神及外道诸魔, 表示驱魔除障。

Pictures of the *Life Story of Sakyamuni*. The murals on the eastern and western side walls painted in colour and gold record 34 episodes in the course of Sakyamun's transformation from a Bodhisattva into a Buddha.

法轮殿内的壁画《释迦牟尼本生图》。绘于东西山墙上，采用彩绘描金法，共计34段内容，分别记述了释迦牟尼从多世菩萨到成佛的全过程。

The lama orchestra performing in Yonghegong.
雍和宫的僧人乐队

◁ The Terraced City of Baisaajya. The Terraced City, also known as Mandra, is a place where the Buddhas cultivate themselves in the Buddhist truth and a Buddhist paradise. It is generally depicted in plane drawings or with three-dimensional models or a group of buildings. The Terraced City of Baisajya is the place where Baisajya Buddha cultivates himself and his world.

药师佛坛城。坛城又称曼陀罗，是诸佛修行的场所，也为佛教理想中的极乐世界，一般以平面图、立体模型以及建筑形式来表现。药师佛坛城即是表现药师佛修行的场所或药师佛所在的世界。

Kabuyang Tubudan, the abbot of Yonghegong.
雍和宫住持加木杨·吐布丹

The lamas in Yonghegong.
雍和宫的僧侣们

The newly re-gilded giant Buddha ▷
shines with splendid lustre.
重新贴金之后,大佛通体金光灿然。

During a religious ritual in Yonghegong, sacred food, which symbolizes happiness and blessing, is distributed among believers.

雍和宫举行佛事活动期间，向信众布施圣食，象征将幸福、吉祥垂赐人间。

Dressed in robes, the lamas come to worship the Buddha and recite scriptures in the Hall of the Wheel of the Dharma every day in the early morning. On religious festivals and memorial days, Buddhist activities and rituals are held in this hall.

法轮殿内的佛事活动。每天清晨，僧侣们都要身穿法衣到该殿中礼拜、诵经，逢有宗教节日或纪念日都要在这里举行佛事活动和法会。

A ceremony for enshrining the Buddha is held during the incinerating ceremony.

在"烧施"法会上，正进行迎请佛仪式。

The incinerating ceremony is in progress. ▷
"烧施"法会正在进行。

63

The Devil-Catching Ceremony is an important religious ceremony held every year in Yonghegong. Lasting three days, the ceremony includes religious dances performed by lamas with a mysterious touch and is watched by a large number of spectators. Picture shows lamas performing the Sitolin Dance.

"打鬼"是雍和宫每年一度重要的宗教仪式,前后共三天,主要内容是僧侣们进行佛教舞蹈表演,充满神秘色彩,场面热闹非凡。图为"跳尸陀林舞"。

A mask for the Sitolin Dance, one of the masks worn in the performances at the Devil-Catching Ceremony.

"打鬼"面具之一,尸陀林舞面具。

A mask for the Dance of the Guardian of the Law, one of the masks worn in the performances at the Devil-Catching Ceremony.

"打鬼"面具之一,护法神舞面具。

Another mask for the Dance of the Guardian of the Law, one of the masks worn in the performances at the Devil-Catching Ceremony.
"打鬼"面具之一,跳护法神舞时所戴的面具。

The figure of Toma, the devil to be eliminated, is burned at the end of the Devil-Catching Ceremony.

"打鬼"时除祟朵马造型。"打鬼"结束时要将其焚化。

The ceremony for sending off evils is held by the lamas led by the abbot near the end of the performances at the Devil-Catching Ceremony.

"打鬼"表演接近尾声、众僧侣在住持的带领下举行送祟仪式。

The Devil-Catching Ceremony ends with the lamas lining up in the courtyard of arches outside the Gate of Luminous Peace for the evil-dispatching incineration.

全寺僧侣列队在昭泰门外的牌楼院送祟焚化,"打鬼"仪式遂告结束。

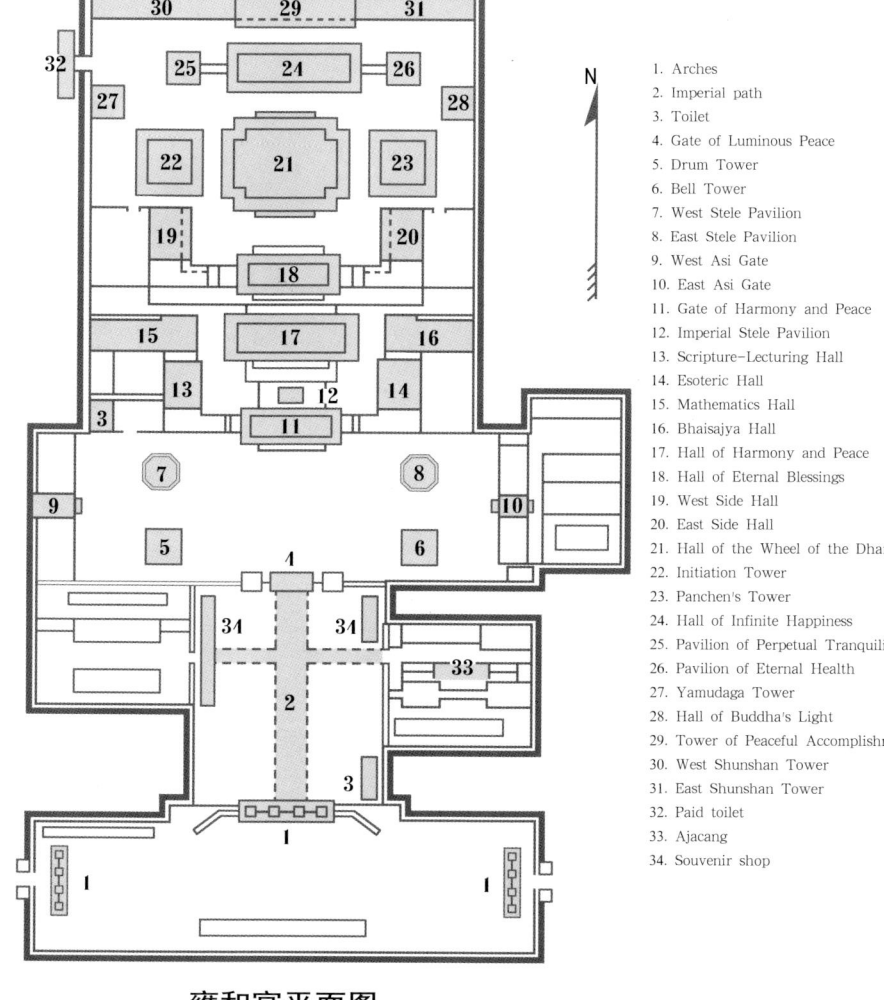

雍和宫平面图
PLANE FIGURE TO LAMASERY OF HARMONY AND PEACE

1. 牌楼
2. 辇道
3. 公厕
4. 昭泰门
5. 鼓楼
6. 钟楼
7. 西碑亭
8. 东碑亭
9. 西阿斯门
10. 东阿斯门
11. 雍和门
12. 四体碑亭
13. 讲经殿
14. 密宗殿
15. 数学殿
16. 药师殿
17. 雍和宫殿
18. 永佑殿
19. 西配殿
20. 东配殿
21. 法轮殿
22. 戒台楼
23. 班禅楼
24. 万福阁
25. 延绥阁
26. 永康阁
27. 雅木达嘎楼
28. 照佛楼
29. 绥成楼
30. 西顺山楼
31. 东顺山楼
32. 收费厕所
33. 阿嘉仓
34. 卖品部

1. Arches
2. Imperial path
3. Toilet
4. Gate of Luminous Peace
5. Drum Tower
6. Bell Tower
7. West Stele Pavilion
8. East Stele Pavilion
9. West Asi Gate
10. East Asi Gate
11. Gate of Harmony and Peace
12. Imperial Stele Pavilion
13. Scripture-Lecturing Hall
14. Esoteric Hall
15. Mathematics Hall
16. Bhaisajya Hall
17. Hall of Harmony and Peace
18. Hall of Eternal Blessings
19. West Side Hall
20. East Side Hall
21. Hall of the Wheel of the Dharma
22. Initiation Tower
23. Panchen's Tower
24. Hall of Infinite Happiness
25. Pavilion of Perpetual Tranquility
26. Pavilion of Eternal Health
27. Yamudaga Tower
28. Hall of Buddha's Light
29. Tower of Peaceful Accomplishment
30. West Shunshan Tower
31. East Shunshan Tower
32. Paid toilet
33. Ajacang
34. Souvenir shop

图书在版编目(CIP)数据

雍和宫:英汉对照/吴文编。—北京:外文出版社,1999.6
ISBN 7-119-02393-4

Ⅰ.雍… Ⅱ.吴… Ⅲ.雍和宫-概况-英.汉 Ⅳ.K928.75
中国版本图书馆 CIP 数据核字(1999)第 16905 号

Compiled by:Wu Wen
Text by:Danjiong Rannabanza   Li Decheng
　　　　　Wu Wen
Consultants:Kabuyang Tubudan   Luosang Samadan
Edited by:Wei Aijun
Photos by:Du Dianwen   Feng Changyi
　　　　　Zhang Zhaoji   Liu Fengzhen
　　　　　Gong Yi
Translated by:Tang Bowen
Designed by:Yuan Qing

编辑:吴　文
撰稿:丹迥·冉纳班杂　李德成　吴　文
顾问:加木杨·吐布丹　罗桑·撒马丹
摄影:杜殿文　冯长义　张肇基
　　　刘凤珍　宫　艺
翻译:汤博文
责任编辑:韦爱君
设计:元　青

雍和宫

吴　文编

Ⓒ 外文出版社
外文出版社出版
(中国北京百万庄大街 24 号)
邮政编码 100037
外文出版社网页:http://www.flp.com.cn
外文出版社电子邮件地址:info @ flp.com.cn
　　　　　　　　　　　sales @ flp.com.cn
深圳麟德电脑设计制作有限公司电脑制版制作
天时印刷(深圳)有限公司印刷
1999 年(24 开)第一版
1999 年第一版第一次印刷
(英汉)
ISBN 7-119-02393-4/J·1505(外)
004800 (精)

First Edition 1999

Lamasery of Harmony and Peace

ISBN 7-119-02393-4

Ⓒ Foreign Languages Press
Published by Foreign Languages Press
24 Baiwanzhuang Road,Beijing 100037,China
Home Page:http://www.flp.com.cn
E-mail Addresses:info @ flp.com.cn
　　　　　　　　sales @ flp.com.cn
Printed in the People's Republic of China